All Things Work Together

All Things Work Together

It's Gonna Be All Right

By
Peter Keese

RESOURCE *Publications* • Eugene, Oregon

ALL THINGS WORK TOGETHER
It's Gonna Be All Right

Copyright © 2025 Peter Keese. All rights reserved. Except for brief quotations in critical publications or reviews, no part of this book may be reproduced in any manner without prior written permission from the publisher. Write: Permissions, Wipf and Stock Publishers, 199 W. 8th Ave., Suite 3, Eugene, OR 97401.

Resource Publications
An Imprint of Wipf and Stock Publishers
199 W. 8th Ave., Suite 3
Eugene, OR 97401

www.wipfandstock.com

PAPERBACK ISBN: 979-8-3852-4006-7
HARDCOVER ISBN: 979-8-3852-4007-4
EBOOK ISBN: 979-8-3852-4008-1

VERSION NUMBER 012925

And I dedicate this book to Helen, to our two wonderful children and their wonderful children, and my siblings, in-laws, students, parishioners, Christ Church, Rugby, long-time close friends, Mystic Knights—in short, all the people I've encountered through my lifetime who've shared their lives and enriched mine.

TO LIFE

When we are no longer able to change a situation,
we are challenged to change ourselves.

Viktor Frankl

Things are not all as graspable and sayable
as on the whole we are led to believe;
most events are unsayable, occur in a
space that no word has ever penetrated.

Letters to a Young Poet, Rainer, Maria Rilke

We don't quit playing because we grow old,
we grow old because we quit playing.

George Bernard Shaw

Contents

Acknowledgments | xi

It's Gonna Be All Right | 1
The Sermon | 3
One | 5
1. Learning Empathy | 7
2. Second Nature | 9
Trust the Process | 10
Skills and Souls | 11
Observer/observed | 12
Cancer | 13
Entanglement | 14
Reality | 15
Reality Part 2 | 16
Creation | 17
No One Was Looking | 19
Hamartia | 20
A Drink, Painting, Watching the Sunset | 21
My Creed Revisited | 22
God and Donald | 24
Jesus and Charlie Brown | 25
The Message | 26
Looking for Jesus | 27
Hazard | 28
The Jesus Movement | 29
Mystery | 30

Truth | 31
Nun-such | 32
Eliminate | 33
Human Nature | 34
Good and Evil | 35
Crying for Bull Conner | 36
Idol Worship (or The Jews Are Right) | 37
The Magic Sword | 38
Miss Fiske | 39
Delicated | 40
I Used to Be Somebody | 41
Nuance | 43
Touching | 44
Baby's Breath | 45
In Time | 46
Cormac | 47
I Have Seen God | 48
Spring | 49
What We Can't Allow | 50
Francis | 52
Sanguine | 53
Mindfulness | 54
The Grown-ups | 55
Black Prisoners Face Higher Rate of Botched Executions, Study Finds | 56
Life is Beautiful | 57
Pockador | 60
All Things Work Together | 61
All Things Work Together—Part 2 | 62
Who Is on Your Kill List? | 64
Ella | 66

My Creed Revisited | 67
Possibilities | 68
Robin and the Man From the Bridge | 69
The Intersection | 71
The Order | 72
Twenty-Five | 73
Friends? | 74
Letting Go | 75
What Jesus Said | 77
On Reading Mary Oliver at 86 | 78
Celebrant | 80
Favorites | 81
Black and White Together | 83
Two Broods | 84
Eighty | 86
And So It Goes | 88
At the Dinner Table | 89
Here's How It Works | 90
'Black Holes Ain't So Black' | 91
Strawberry Moon | 93
Ramiro Gonzales | 94
Nourishment | 95
A Twofer | 96
Do We Need A President? | 97
The Role | 98
I Want Both | 100
Levitate | 101
Church | 102
The Dating Service | 104
Comedy | 105
Jesus Reads Emily Post | 107

Defining G-d | 108
A Debate | 110
July 4 | 112
Angels | 113
Bluewater | 114
Tears | 116
It's Never Just a Sheet | 119
Onomatopoeia | 120
A Turning Point | 121
A Widower's Epiphany | 122
Ode to the Krystal | 123
Hospitality | 125
A Morning | 126
A Drought | 127
The Rain Comes | 128
I Gave up Golf Today | 129
Filigree | 131
Good Enough | 132
This Is the World | 133
In the Garden on a Sunday Morning | 134
The Sheet | 135
Innocent | 136
The Rock | 137
Power | 138
The Ants and the Alcoholic | 139
Confront | 140
Riches | 142
Longing | 143

Acknowledgments

Chris, Cathy, Rick and Ginny, my writer's group Scribblers (especially Anne and Dana), and my editor, Aemilia, have all read some or all of what I've written, and, in every case, have improved what I wrote. I am a novice, learning to be a poet. My gratitude to these and my many other teachers is beyond measure.

It's Gonna Be All Right

The world's in terrible shape
bombing, starvation, murder, rape

don't worry,
it's gonna be all right

are you not listening?
not paying attention?
how justify this invention
your
"all is good" proclivity?
Have you toxic positivity?

naw, honey, I ain't got that

but I remember that lady
with an 'issue of blood'
who crept up and stood
behind Jesus and was cured

I remember
he said,
I didn't do it
it was your
trusting spirit

as Julian said,
all shall be well
or, it's gonna be all right,
as I say
or as my friend says,
I'm not OK,
you're not Ok,
but that's OK

it's gonna be all right

The Sermon

A homily I'll likely not
ever preach:

One:
The truth will set you free

Two:
There is no life after
neither heaven nor hell
though plenty of both
right here now

Three:
God and process
one and the same
real and indefinable

Four:
blood sacrifice is an
ancient superstition
the notion that Jesus' blood
saves you is first cousin to that
it has no validity

Five:
Getting together to share
food and drink is good in itself—
and creates and celebrates
community
the notion that we are
eating a body, drinking blood
is not necessary

Six:
There is evil in your heart
there is good in your heart
you have some choice in
the matter

Seven:
Everybody experiences trauma
it is no excuse

Eight:
Happiness and sadness
are both conditions of
human existence

Nine:
Playing is good

Ten:
You can choose to believe that
it will be all right, and
all shall be well

One

Miniscule it may be
but not thereby
without significance

meditating this morning
as accustomed, I "ohmmm..."
and feel the hum of it
throughout my body
comforted by the
sense, hope, trust
that my hum is
in harmony with
the hum of the universe

miniscule—the difference
between me and animal,
vegetable, grass, fungi
yet signifying the
importance of each
separately, to choose
to acknowledge...

one of my best teachers
ever, Jim Hardie,
working with deeply regressed
patients in a large mental hospital,

gently holds the patient's
hand, touches his arm,
and says, "This is you."
Then, touching his own,
"This is me."
He repeats this
several times

holding hands
"this is you"
"this is me"

One

1. Learning Empathy

There are many aspects
many discrete steps,
if you think about it,
in learning empathy.

In effort to define them
we're beyond elaboration
in a state of expatiation

Ockham and others suggest
we might in fact do best
to simplify

it's the process
of learning
by being and doing

So I guess you'll have to
get in bed with your patient.
(*pace*, friend—a metaphor here;
and you'll learn soon enough
how close to adhere.)

for example
Emma narrates:
"my favorite professor,
demanding as she was,
as I lay dying,
near my last breath,
pulled her chair up close and
read me a story
The Runaway Bunny
then she slipped
under the covers
next to me.

And, when it was time,
she got back out of bed
put on her coat
picked up her bag
and left the room."*

---

* Suggested by a scene from the movie, *Wit*, starring Emma Thompson.

2. Second Nature

A quiet young man
serious demeanor

a friend comes to him
with a sadness
he attends, and
she is comforted

not something you
might normally expect
from a male
and so young.

He the only male
of the six siblings
the youngest two
severely mentally
and physically
limited twins

second nature

Trust the Process

We are in a travel van
to get from here to there
we accomplish our plan

the place seems wondrous
we gather to process
the journey and the 'van'
the transport and its state

did the driver know the way?
we were not always sure
there were some heavy jolts
potholes and such
and death, grief, anger, and much
much more

our daily huddle in that bus—
the process
of joining
created us
our life together, our
fighting and our hugs
it was the very process
that we were learning
and doing together

process
indefinable
knowable only
in the doing
happens in
journeying together.

Skills and Souls

There's a story about Jesus
it's in the Bible and may be true
a young man asks, "what must I do?"

calls to mind a more recent story
also possibly true
about another young man,
and "what must I do?"

both young lads were truly good boys
they come to the master
one a master teacher,
the other a master builder
boys don't brag, but list their abilities
"I've obeyed all the rules."
"I'm a very accomplished carpenter"
"so what must I do," each inquired
"to complete my goodness?"

Teacher: "wonderful, so good to hear;
I am very proud of you, but, be clear
none of that counts toward goodness"

Master builder: "I've watched you work
truly you're a fine carpenter, but . . .
your busyness makes you lose
those many chances to schmooz
with your team-mates
your skills don't amount to anything
without them."

Observer/observed

who are you?
and where do you stand?

I'm the observer
some distance
from the thing at hand

perhaps not so far
as you fancy, my friend
might it be that
you wish to forefend

in the rich intertwined
world called quantum
"everything is what it is
only with respect
to something else"

the thing happened.
by your observing it
you are participant
in the happening
entangled intertwined
interdependent
observer observed
equal partners
neither is
without the other

ubuntu
entanglement

Cancer

In the wisdom book is written,
"a time to be born, a time to die"
biology and genetics later agree.
It denies wisdom
to give lie to this decree

the rules, you crab, seem not to know
even though it has ever been so;
we rejoice at your time on stage
but when time comes,
you must turn the page.

crab sometimes holds sway
refusing, he asserts his way
sustains his life by consuming yours
you die, he endures
until . . .

the wisdom speaker reaffirms
the immutable truth
and nature confirms

you refuse when it is your time
but your victory is brief
as a parasite you mime
my life, and so we die
together

scorpion and frog

Entanglement

Where and when I don't recall
event itself I remember all
stickerly vine so tightly clings
to base and branch and sings
its parasitic song

with gloves I grasp up and below
my goal, prevent it to grow
remove it clean away
denying forever its sway

great effort, I prevail
or so I think, until
the roots, no avail
they are married, entwined;
again the vine will thrive

meditating this morning
this all comes to me
every thing of every kind we see
entangled, interdependent, not free
clipping and pruning perhaps
as when cancer fails to lapse

but even it manifests what's true
you live off of me and I off of you

Reality

He says, humans are good

Yes, I say

He says, humans are evil

Yes, I say

He says, those two statements are contradictory

They seem so, I say

He says, life is

Yes, I say

He says, death is

Yes, I say

He says, those two things are contradictory

They seem so, I say

He asks, how can it be?

You see that leaf at the base of the tree?
he asks, is it alive or dead?

Yes, I say

Reality Part 2

J. S. Mill once declared this truth
if your own side is all you know
you know little of that, forsooth

Creation

Composer/conductor Leonard Bernstein
with the New York Philharmonic
is exploring creation
Beethoven, Bach, Glenn Gould,
Eileen Farrell, Igor Stravinski

Genesis, 2 and 3, came to mind
as I listened to Leonard lecture
Beethoven putting musical notes
on paper, with almost no direction.
Leo: two different masters
lead the players
to present the music
with such different flavors
one *vivace con brio*
the other *andante cantabile con moto*

who determines
is it Beethoven?
he barely gives a hint
is it the Conductor's whim
or do composer and conductor
have to swim
with one another in concert?

then Gould, and Bach,
who gives a bit more direction
they still have to maintain
conversation, since Johann
is only part of the creative task
Glenn also has his say in
bringing the notes to bask
in glory and beauty

Eileen sings a beautiful song
composer: *allegro vivace e con brio*,
Eileen and he negotiate
her interpretation and his notes
together spring aria to life

some think Genesis names creator
as the only important player
what he wants determines
it all—no question
but as Leonard clearly knows
god may put notes on paper
and even some directions pose
(*"fruit from every tree except that one"*)
but once the performers are on stage
all bets are off and
together they engage
to bring the thing to life

no longer his nor only hers
not puppets nor puppiters—
but equals in the creative work.

No One Was Looking

"As no one was looking
for an 8th planet" said the
article "one was not found."

you see, Uranus didn't move
as astronomers could prove
it should, as it tracked its run
around the sun

it wobbles and pauses
we wonder the causes
could it possibly be
gravity?

there has to be another planet
exerting its strong force
we can't see but we guess a
Neptune setting the course

The great Richard Feynman
knew there is more out there
than he had ever thought of;
he went looking for it
and found so much
that we didn't know
we were looking for.
Carl Sagan says,
"Somewhere, something
incredible is waiting
to be known."

Hamartia

The truth simple and stark
you have missed the mark
bend the bow, let fly
often arrow passes by

here's remedy for this sin:
just try again

remorse and guilt are not needed
they both should go unheeded
the message here is let them go
forgiveness the synonym just so

the miss occurred, can't be denied
shame and guilt are wrongly applied
it is just our nature, the way we are
often to aim, shoot, and miss so far

shame guilt not required
look it up and you will know
forgiveness simply means 'let go'

A Drink, Painting, Watching the Sunset

this watercolorist with such
talent her scenes still link
my heart to her and the beach
where her favorite thing
at the close of the day
was to watch the sunset
and the light fade away.

this line:
"a drink, painting, watching the sunset"
was a spontaneous exclamation
from granddaughter Alex
one evening not long ago
and I thought:
poem

My Creed Revisited

what I wrote some time ago
I still hold as assuredly so:

"Universal life force
surrounds and inheres
energizes all
morally neutral
all powerful"

but . . .

my creed is so bloodless!
no powerful fathergod
with a bleeding savior son
and a motherwise spirit
no drama, no music
no dance—no life!

in his senior years,
author Alec Williamson
begins to study basic math.

he tells of beginning to discover
god
through algebra and geometry

"math is rife with intimations of
a divine presence"
this is not new to mathematicians
ancient and modern, Alec tells us.

"discoveries that mathematicians make
are a mapping of an independent
and timeless territory
a sort of parallel world
where nothing is good or evil
but everything is true."*

A marvelous statement about
an indefinable something/someone—
indefinable,
but not unfelt;
bigger than
good and evil;
and everything true
everything comprehended
and comprehensive
and undefined
and indefinable
and intertwined.

---

* Alec Williamson, "Math Is the Answer to More Than One Question," *New York Times*, Feb. 9, 2024.

God and Donald

Quoth God
"oh, Donald, Donald, how often
would I have made the right sound
for you to hear that like mother hen
I wanted to gather you in my ken

"bigly today you left the court house
your heavy overcoat a shroud
you pump your fist so proud
and I recalled another crowd
the pharisees and saduccees
parading so importantly
in robes for all to see

"I felt about you as I did them
so very, very sad
I saw a forlorn little lad
oh, Donnie, Donnie"

Jesus and Charlie Brown

I wonder if the Lucyworld
promised Jesus
that if he would just be
a good person demonstrating
love and truth-telling,
that she really would hold
that ball for him to kick
through the goalposts

or, year after year
would she promise
and then pull it back
and laugh to see him
fall flat?

Did Jesus know that
he could count on
Lucyworld to do
what she always did
and yet still decide
to kick that ball anyway?

Why would he do that?

The Message

2/16/24

is often not clear to me.

then Alexei Navalny died
in prison today

he came
back to his beloved country
to demonstrate freedom
his mine yours

not, like most Christians
(me, included),
only *preaching* that
you are FREE
and powerful thereby

but to demonstrate
what freedom and
power look like

Looking for Jesus

I know right where to find Jesus
close your eyes and take my hand
now walk with me
and turn this way

now open your eyes
you are staring in a mirror
whose face do you see?

just so

oh, it's Buddha you seek?
I know right where to find the Buddha
close your eyes and . . .
well, you get the drift

so is that all there is to it?

oh no; it is just
the beginning of the all

Hazard

Hazard—danger ahead—says the sign
just ahead is the little town in
eastern Kentucky—a once thriving coal town

some say that when coal left
the town died and only the maggots
remained, the dealers and the
clinics who pretended to treat
those addicted, with more pills

a corpse of a town
then

a few years ago a 42 y.o. citizen,
a former addict who loved to read
opened a small bookstore
another former addict opened
a clothing store

171 former addicts with jobs
in the newly opening local stores
toy store, smoothie shop, restaurant
43 businesses have begun—all local

Perhaps this poem should be titled
Easter

The Jesus Movement

is rampant in the Episcopal Church these days
one more expression of the basic ways
to preach the Christian theme—Jesus is alive

I have two things to say to that

one: Jesus is dead as a drowned rat

two: I believe in life, death, and resurrection

Mystery

"Master," said the pupil
"you often speak of mystery
what is mystery?"

Master did not speak.

it would be a mistake
to think that
he did not reply.

Truth

The propagandist
intends to convince you
that what she says is THE truth

John presents the propagandist
"I am the way, the truth, and the life
you can't get there any other
way except through me."

I am so grateful that
Jesus never said that

Nun-such

She slaps his hand
sharply
with a big ruler

he learns
that behavior
is not approved

now at 73
the big ruler
is not necessary
to remind him

and his verbal disdain
of the foolish rigidity
only proves how
powerfully formative
those early years are

I observe this from
outside his culture
and then I think

I can see it happen in him
and I begin to wonder
what early experiences
so powerfully formed me

who is my nun?

Eliminate

Ex limen, literally
from the threshold

The candidate for Bishop
declares her intent to
eliminate racism
kick it from the threshold

can you do that without
kicking the racist out?

destroy the village to save it?

'hate the sin
but love the sinner'?

can the two be separated?

Sin—a morally neutral term
to describe the nature
of human nature—

has taken on a negative cast
flawed—bad—morally corrupt

but consider . . .

sometimes the flaw may be
good, rich, imaginative, creative

Human Nature

Many years ago a bright student
gave me a saying I thought she
attributed to an eastern sage.
Maybe she made it up
I can't find it in any page
but of course that won't stop
me from quoting it here

in a wonderful discussion
the other day, the topic of
human ability to change
became the focus for a time

Later I thought of this made-up
eastern philosopher saying
"Do you think you can change
the world? It can't be done
It is perfect as it is"

Good and Evil

everything is ultimately good
evil only a temporary condition

or does evil have
equal rank with good?

I have a friend who
thinks we invent evil
so we can feel good

Rumi imagines a field beyond
right-doing and wrong-doing
where he wants to lie down
with you,
where even the notion
of you and me as separate is
non-sensical

trying to define God,
is just like the question,
is there a field beyond?

Crying for Bull Conner

A little black boy in
Birmingham marches
for freedom

Bull says, "what do you
want, nigger?"
Freeman says
"we want to kneel
to pray for freedom"

Bull Conner spits
on him
and puts him in jail

Freeman was bitter for years

he tells of the day
many years later when
Bull Conner died

Freeman's mother calls, crying.

"why're you crying for that man?"

"because he was a mother's child
and she never taught him to love"

Freeman cried too
and the bitterness washed away.*

---

* Based on Tad Walch, "The Lesson in Love and Hate a Mother Taught Her Wronged Son," *Deseret News*, Mar. 4, 2024. Dr. Freeman A. Hrabowski III (b. 1950) was president of University of Maryland, Baltimore, from 1992 to 2022.

Idol Worship (or The Jews Are Right)

There is only one, say the Jews
and that is the one to call
as our only true muse

A Rabbi friend years ago
kindly helped me know

yet there's a problem you see
it is that they are not free
to use the holy one's name
G–D, YHWH
the closest they came

because

GOD
is an idol with
shape and form,
definition, limit

so

trust the process
which is limitless

The Magic Sword

I'm only human, we say
most often on the day
we're caught in the wrong

And, if church is our kin
we use the word sin
without worry at all
that thus we will fall

because we've been shriven
forever forgiven
god's work alone
means that ours is
eternal salvation

we've confessed
and also professed
Jesus as lord
the magic sword
against all evil

Miss Fiske

The creative Miss Fiske
in 1814 did begin
Young Ladies' Seminary in
Keene, New Hampshire

Her goal:
"to qualify woman
to think with candor
act with justice
counsel with kindness
direct with wisdom."

The prophet Micah
in 800 BC did set
this goal for all to get:
do justice
love kindness
live humbly

wisdom endures
from age to age

Delicated

A section in Betsy Cox's
magnificent book, Van Gogh
gives a delightful riff on
cause and effect

confusion, inaccurate memory
leads to a joyful effect
Betsy's book inspires in me

A few pages later, my eyes
misread a word as "delicated"
when what she said was
tree trunks were "delineated"
by rain
delicated isn't a word–
until now–but
can't you just picture
a delicated rain pattern?

I Used to Be Somebody

On the waterfront,
Terry laments to his brother
"I coulda been somebody;
I coulda been a contendah"*
those word come to me now

And I see
that very longing to be
somebody, in these latter
days of my retirement

Terry says he's just a bum;
these days that's not my sum
these days I'm just invisible
people used to see me
I used to be somebody

When I was somebody
people would seek me
I had worth
I was worth

this new day requires
a new ploy
to find the joy
of my wisdom
being sought

---

* From the movie made in 1954, starring Marlon Brando.

I shall seek Hyde Park square
and stand there and share
I'll frame my thought
to inspire yours, too

Like Socrates and companions
shaping new opinions

Nuance

old man listening
young ones surround
they have no doubt
their certainty abounds

he does not speak.
he thinks, "yes, but
maybe there's more
to the matter—
some nuance"

he's still a participant
should he share his
observation?

Touching

The morning she died
I was helping her dress
she in her chair
behind her, I am
massaging her shoulders

somehow anew that day
enjoying flesh on flesh
I thought
I'll do this every morning.

She had her seizure
later that morning
and was conscious
no more

Up until the last
the joy of learning
ways
to know and love
Helen

Baby's Breath

Helen died four years ago
daughter, Kate, commemorated
with a bouquet of flowers
gift to me on the date.

flowers have long since expired

except baby's breath
standing guard
keeping watch

I catch my breath
gratitude

In Time

The little bunny rabbit
sits just a few feet away

is he proud—or scared?
maybe both

I want us to be friends

talking to him
doesn't seem to work
he has his own language
it is not mine
at least, not initially

sit quietly, observe
listen
in time, perhaps
tell him what you
see and hear

and maybe he'll tell you

Cormac

A novelist dark
has a character profess
his thoughts about evil

the fact about it
is that no one says a bit
about evil—its fame
we give it no name
we ignore it
we don't know
how to speak of
something that is
nothing

"you ain't nothin"
kid says to the murderer,
the life-long killer
without conscience,
who says in return,

"You speak truer
than you know"*

---

* Cormac McCarthy, *Blood Meridian, Or the Evening Redness in the West* (New York: Modern Library, 2001), 345.

I Have Seen God

She is beauty absolute
I've not actually seen "God"
but I don't mean to refute
her beauty

Quantum physicist Carl Rovelli[*]
is setting my heart on fire
with what does inspire
my desire to shout with
the joy of the life
he describes as rife
with rich entanglement
life-enhancing interdependence

*"this magical light-flooded
kaleidoscope in which
we are amazed to exist
and that we call our world."*

Beauty absolute

---

[*] Carlo Rovelli, *Helgoland* (New York: Penguin, 2022), 112 (Kindle).

Spring

4/7

My first day this year
to sit outside and read
wind chimes sing as I sit

I look up
"hello there, young tree
proudly swaying so free
your golden crown alight
and so very bright
newly garbing yourself in
your budding summer dress"

Daughter Kate was born
Nana arrives that very day
"she'll look so much
better with clothes on"
family lore ever after.

I recall that now
my tree friend did look
unclothed when she shed
last fall
but not less beautiful

And still I rejoice to see
her dance and garb
after her winter rest

What We Can't Allow

Ukraine gives Russia its identity
Russia becomes Russia
borrowing Kiev's life and religion
making them its own

black people give the US its identity
the US becomes the U.S.
depending on their life
which life becomes its own

Russia needs Ukraine,
but...
it needs Ukraine not to be;
its existence an embarrassment

The US would not exist without
its black folks
but...
it needs its them not to be;
their existence an embarrassment

Ukraine is not a real thing,
but...
here it is
in our history
and our now

Black people are not a real thing
but . . .
here they are
in our history
and our now

Francis

Was Joseph Pharoah's puppet?
One could easily think so
the ruler set him free of jail
made him prime to prevail

was he then owned or free?
how is a man to be
"his own man," as they say
when he is under the sway
of Pharoah?

Some see Francis as emperor
The Pharoah of this modern day
or is he owned by the empire
unless he finds a way
to speak free and true?

Francis speaks of two:
"laboratory faith"
and "journey faith"
the one, theories
the other, lived
he favors the lived, but
sits on Church's throne,
the lab his domain

can he—can we
live in the lab and also be
pilgrims on the journey
living the life?

Sanguine

bright red blood
signifies
that it is good—
oxygen-filled

so marvelous
the heart pumps away
blood nourishing
the farthest toe

blood, exhausted
turns pale and
makes its way
back home

where the heart is

lungs do their good
re-oxygenate the blood
it becomes sanguine
again

life renews

Mindfulness

I'm not sure what it means
to me it says pay attention
accompanied by
a little embarrassment
when it reminds me how
impoverished I am, as in
that old country joke,
I'm so poor I can't
even pay attention

my attending has its own mind
it wanders here and there
and occasionally
I'm jolted by awareness
I'm standing here, but
my mind is not
and I can't begin to tell you
what is going on here
or there . . .
I remind myself
look, listen,
touch, smell
taste

The Grown-ups

walking through the lobby
with my boss, a regular event
a colleague stops to talk
he and George engage
I stand right there
but wander away

later, the epiphany

I'm walking with my father
a friend stops to talk
he and my Daddy engage
I'm there but . . .
I have no idea what they said

When the grown-ups stop to talk
the kid stands silent

Black Prisoners Face Higher Rate of Botched Executions, Study Finds

(NYT, 4/18/24)

"Botched" says it all
take one step back—don't fall

from this perspective
it is nothing but surreal
that we truly believe
and solemnly declare

a need for better research
how to kill people
more efficiently
and effectively

do we not recall that
there were some folks
in first half of last century
who developed some expertise
in the matter?

Life is Beautiful*

Guido and his friend—
are they fools
as in medieval days?
that's how they appear
as the story purveys
many improbable events
Guido, in his clownish
and naïve ways
in whom there is no guile
exudes a charm
that wins the girl
and they have a son

(he wins the girl away
from a pompous man
in uniform whose scowl
hints of things to come)

magic tricks
madcap adventures
laughter, joy
the boy is given
a tank for a toy

gradually we begin to see
we are in fascist Italy
in the late 1930s

---

* An Italian movie, made in 1997.

Papa, why aren't Jews allowed?
he winks, it's all part of the game

Guido's sunny disposition remains
is he just simple and stupidly optimistic?
No, he refuses to let clouds hide the sun

We see the many clouds
Guido and the boy are
herded on to the train
wife/momma frantic
insists that she ride too
at the camp she's sent
with the women
boy cries out "Momma"
she reaches out
but is dragged away

In the grim barracks
Guido keeps the game
"stay quiet, hide here
whoever first gets to a
thousand points will
win the prize—a tank!"

Then . . .

Allies have won
they approach camp
Axis soldiers slink away
Guido hides the boy safe to stay
"don't come out until all is silent,
and you'll win the prize"

the last departing Axis guard
　　　shoots and Guido dies

　　　　　silence

　　　the boy comes out
　　as the American tank
　　　rounds the corner

mouth *O*—eyes wide—joy!

Riding with the soldier on top
he sees, and cries out, "Momma"

　　finally a retrospect
　　what we've seen
　　is the adult son's
　　remembrance of how
　　Papa saved his life
and he's reunited with Momma

　　　Life is beautiful

Pockador

Daddy, what's a pockador?

I don't know, son; what is it?

But, Dad, you told me that
we have one hiding in our house

Oh, yes, I remember now
it is a straaange animal
that is big, tall and thin
and it keeps people
separate from one another
when it is out

Sam, you shouldn't tease him

Oh, he'll learn soon enough
what a pocket door is

All Things Work Together

for good, so the book claims;
but the fine print proclaims
the reward limits to
"those who love God"

I like to think wider
that the provider
is as universal in view
as *all* does imply

could we "God" excise
and so make the prize
simply available to all
who love?

so there'd still be a condition
just not beyond our rendition

All Things Work Together—Part 2

for good, it says—

until they don't

she called me yesterday
hosting a "pity party" she said
and it was
she's good at it

she's made a mess
drugs, alcohol, divorces
she's got a mouth on her
and she's bright, clever
sensitive, attentive, and funny

she called from her hospital bed
she's having a transfusion
her hemoglobin is low
"that means my body is
attacking itself; why is that?"

of course she has her own
explanation, being deep
in the Baptist tradition—
it is punishment for
all her wickedness

since I got my degree
from divinity school
all I could tell her is
"your theology is
all fucked up"

trust Guido

Who Is on Your Kill List?

People convicted of
first degree murder
for sure

*oh, I'm against taking
any life for any reason*

so, the fertilized egg?

*don't use that sophistry
on me
that's no human life*

don't use that big word
on me
that's just your denial
life is life from the beginning

*yes, until it ends—
with the state's execution*

so you would destroy fetus
or an eight-week one
if it is deformed or
a danger to mother?

the murderer has taken
a life
it is only just that he
gives one in return

we are both killers
you and I
you have your reason
I have mine

a character in Verghese's novel
offers this perspective:
"if there's a fire in my house
and I must choose between
my husband and my clay pot
well all I can say is . . .
he's lived a good life"*

---

* Abraham Verghese, *Covenant of Water* (New York: Grove Atlantic, 2023), 642.

Ella[*]

April 26

beautiful hair
a sheen
a glow
a deep rich crown
not a gaudy gold
but a royal purple
shining glory

[*] This person, my grandchild, had their hair dyed yesterday.

My Creed Revisited

Gandhi says
"There are people
in the world
so hungry that
God cannot appear
to them
except in the form
of food."

the question that persists
does God really exist?
might be better expressed
is nourishment available?

that one we can answer.

Possibilities

The seas are rising
an article apprising
then declares that
things are bad and
will only get worse

facts and editorial
often get mixed
seas rising—a fact
"bad" and "worse"
should be nixed
from the news page

the lower countries
years ago
managed those facts
and made it so
that they have flowered

Robin and the Man From the Bridge

longtime I've appreciated
dare I even say loved
the Robin Williams
who has enriched my life
with the humanity he has so
beautifully brought alive
on the screen.

Wildly comic, deeply feeling.
you do remember, don't you,
that he died by his own hand?

That's in mind; it recalls
the powerful, sad, and
beautifully written
story by my comrade,
Dana, my sister-in-law

I never knew the man
on the bridge

In a neighboring county
a bridge over a deep ravine
a man stands on the railing
Dana tells us that he
is a lovely and loved
husband, father, lawyer
accomplished in all

Dana says,
he could have stepped
back down to the pavement
but

"He stepped out
into the blue sky.

"And no one knows why."

and no one knows why

The Intersection

Arthur Erickson, architect
explores, builds on the intersect
the construct and the landscape
the man-made and the natural
The Law Courts in Vancouver
marry the lush hedges and
the glass-encased courts

past and present exist together
each flows out and in the other

Arthur eschews reading about
in order to understand
rather he sits and looks
his knowing to expand

his, ours, to replicate
the beauty that is

The Order

You have to catch them
before you can eat them

you can't count them
before they hatch

cart before the horse
and other such aphorisms
seem not to affect the course
of our beloved church

we want to eat first

Twenty-Five

Almost all of us was sure
twenty-five years ago
that 'traditional' marriage
remained pure,
and same-sex marriage
would not—could not—be.

now seventy plus per cent
accept it as a normal

how did we do that?

if we let it be
will love prevail?

Friends?

They occupy the same space
little rabbits and little squirrels
scampering in our backyard
and I wonder
how they greet one another

or maybe, like elevator occupants
fully aware of one another
they don't look or speak
maybe they exit with

"have a good day."

Letting Go

1

David, young, brash, cocky
I don't speak here of king
this David asks to be
let in to the ring—
certified as one of us
a clinical educator

Years later, we give him
our Distinguished Service Award;
he speaks; he tells of his long
painful journey, how once
even his beginning certification
was taken from him

mellowed now, his acceptance
is warm, witty, wise
and humble

I sit at his table
to give the closing blessing

I was prepared, but . . .

now what can I say
as a member of
the committee that day
which removed his
credentials all the way?
I can't imagine
not mentioning it
but I don't want to . . .

I confess

and then bless

"trust the process"

our mantra

we are so blessed
to let go

2

is a miracle a mirage
a phantasm, a hallucination
is Santa Claus real or
a mirage or a metaphor
or a miracle?

Is there such a thing—
miracle?

is it a miracle that
David's story and mine—
coinciding this night—
allows us to let go
of an old wound?

What Jesus Said

he and some of the boys
had gone on a hike
up the mountain
maybe for a picnic.

sitting around after
bbq beans and beer
do they fall asleep
or hallucinate or fear
when there appear
saints from their past?

Moses and Elijah arrive
and Jesus begins to shine
and the boys hear a voice

then the others are gone
the boys with Jesus alone

impetuous Peter says "WOW"
we need to commemorate now
I know, let's build three grand
tabernacles, one for each

Jesus rolls his eyes
"boy, are you guys slow

"you are the tabernacles"

On Reading Mary Oliver at 86

I never took
to reading poetry as a child,
a boy, a young man, and on

I think I told myself that
I wasn't the kind of person
who reads—who gets—poetry

I'm not talking about
effetes or elites
in fact, I secretly envied those
who seemed to know—
and to speak—
a language I did not know
nor speak

I'm that guy who couldn't
understand why you'd meander
the back road when you
could go straight from
here to there
poetry is not for me

Emily began to break the barrier
when she gently explained
that you can't get
there straight from here
it's always on the slant

so I heed my enthusiastic
friends and go to Mary.
she never says outright
that beauty is everywhere
and in everything

Do you reckon that
Jesus was a naturalist,
like Mary?
maybe what really happened
on that mountain
was that he took some
of the boys on a nature hike
because he and Mary
knew the same secret

Matthew, Mark and Luke
are giving us their slant
on the glory of beauty
and maybe satirizing us
a bit, teasing us for
wanting to enshrine
the shine

Celebrant

Our revered Book of Common Prayer
says the person who presides
at the Eucharist
is "the Celebrant"

that is plain wrong

this one tiny misnaming
hints of the massive error
in our Christian practice

we are the Celebrants
she's merely the president

for want of a nail . . .

Favorites

Jesus took only three
of the twelve
with him to
the mountain top

I immediately assumed
and just as quickly denied
even daring to think
that he was playing favorites

as over the years, I began
to believe and proclaim,
he's simply and only one of us—
human—heir to all the
"slings and arrows"
as Will put it

my mind knows that he is
a man, like me
my heart yearns for more,
surely a good man
doesn't play favorites

men and women,
Jesus among them,
capable of the most
wonderful deeds
of every kind

men and women
also capable of the most
heinous awful hateful deeds
(is Jesus among them?)

Black and White Together

Tears blur my eyes
cloud my vision
as I read James McBride
Miracle at St. Anna[*]

little Italian boy appears
attaches himself to
big Black American soldier
somewhere in Italy
Germans in retreat
still deadly

and my pain
is almost unbearable
mixed with near
indescribable joy
death is near
so is love
little white boy
big black man
each discover
this other one
loves me
and I love him

and the mixing,
the marriage, of
those two inseparables
love and death

---

[*] James McBride, *Miracle at St. Anna* (New York: Riverhead, 2022).

Two Broods

(May–June 2024)

Thirteen and Nineteen
the two broods of cicadas
nineteen emerges every seventeen years
thirteen every thirteen years
the last time they
coincided was in 1803

they appear, they sing
they mate, they die
all in a few weeks span

it's all about love and death
it seems so short,
a puff of breath.

Three score and ten
up against cicada time
may seem to us
an eternal clime

But Will says that life
is shadow, lasting an hour,
and then no more
and the Bible says
it is mist, vapor
a puff of smoke

they accomplish life's
purpose in two weeks
it takes us years

even so it's all the same
love—and death

Eighty

"they looked like logs
floating in the ocean."

a glance at the calendar
this morning, June 6, 2024
reminds me

eighty years ago they came
on to the beach
and fell, so many of them
and some never even
got to the beach
"they looked like logs
floating in the ocean"

just a kid.
one moment
a being;
next
a body

philosophize if you will
there still lies
there lies still
the body
of a being
known,
cherished
no longer being

they knew they might die
yes, like we all know
and don't know
until . . .
we no longer know
anything

D-Day, the 6th of June

And So It Goes

The refrain does
what a refrain does
it repeats

It was his phrase*
every time
a death occurred:
and so it goes

many have discussed
what he meant.
I take it as
acceptance

I started to say
simple acceptance,
but it is not simple.
it is simply full
complete

encompassing
the grief, the joy
the pain, the hope
the reality
that can never be
fully comprehended
I want this to be
the closing phrase
of my obituary

and so it goes

* Kurt Vonnegut, *Slaughterhouse Five* (New York: Delacorte, 1969).

At the Dinner Table

father sits here
mother sits there
at opposite ends
brother brother on one side
sister brother on the other
between parents

they talk
above our heads
is somebody mad?

Shh . . . don't tell anyone
tell anyone what?
we don't talk about it
talk about what?

you know
I don't—what?

we don't talk about
what we don't talk about

Oh
?

Here's How It Works

She tells her story
and so then believes it

and

she believes her story
and so then tells it

people do that

families do that

churches do that

even whole nations do that

'Black Holes Ain't So Black'

All gnarled up
in a motorized wheelchair
speaks via synthesizer
told he would die
in two years—he was twenty-one

*(next two stanzas
to be read
in the cadence
of "Five Foot Two")*

he could not talk
he could not write
but, oh how he could
calculate

black holes suck
everything in
and they never
ever appear again
has anybody seen
light show

until Stephen Hawking
imagined a formula
that purports to show
"black holes ain't so black"
in fact they glow

and he came to know
that all which seemed
forever detained
would some day
appear again

a rich man living a rich life
until at age seventy-six he died
enjoying from his
gnarled position, he
opened our eyes
to a marvelously
rich and beautiful universe

Strawberry Moon

June 21, 2024

granddaughter Ella and I
stand in our backyard
and ooh and sigh

she is big and red
and so nearby

Ramiro Gonzales

June 26, 2024

from an abused childhood
traveled this lonely and
directionless young man

at age 18, he murdered
Bridget Townsend

for the last 18 years
he has lived on death row
until
the State of Texas killed him today

Ramiro is one
who murdered;
is he now indelibly
and forever
only "murderer"?

Maybe it asks too much
of the law to distinguish

By all accounts in these 18 years
he had become one who loved widely,
and experienced and offered mercy,
remorse and forgiveness

Ramiro knew resurrection

can Texas?

Nourishment

It will come.
meditation is all about
letting it come

let what come?

well I won't know
exactly
until it comes

I know that
it pervades
ready to reveal

*passive, then
is mine to be?*

No, actively
attending
receiving
digesting

sit up, friend
and take
nourishment

A Twofer

1.

Scientists and it

True Science believes in it
and is always in search of it
certain that it is exquisite

2.

Scientists and god

some believe fervently
some reluctantly
and some not at all

Do We Need a President?

Yes, declares a New York Times
columnist who goes on to
hint at the definition of the role

but his headline
sets my mind to this:
do we need a god?

and what is god's role?

so, then, I got to imagining . . .

The Role

who better than a gay
process theologian
to speak of god as
"the divine yum yum"

delicious, beautiful, fun
is that the role?
does more need be said?

well yes, it turns out that
More (as in Thomas)
friend to Erasmus
who writes
In Praise of Folly
satirizing the whole
Christian enterprise—
is the more

and later
Karl's elder brother,
Hugo Rahner, writes
Man At Play

Who knew of
the long and deep
investment of the church
in *eutrapelia*—
wittiness,
lighthearted playfulness
(I love to play with words)

God the playful
what a mindful
why even the
most atheistic scientist
can only mindtwist
at the twirling pirouettes
of those little atom-lets

the lord be with you
let us play

I Want Both

Hans Rosling wants
to split the difference
"neither optimist
nor pessimist
just a possibilist"*

satire, Auden said,
is
angry and optimistic
and
comedy is
good-tempered and
pessimistic

both are playful

let's play

---

* Hans Rosling et al., *Factfulness: Ten Reasons We're Wrong About the World—and Why Things Are Better Than You Think* (New York: Flatiron, 2018).

Levitate

Why didn't we call it
levitator instead of elevator?

Hmmm . . .

the words are at least
first cousins if not twins

maybe levitate sounds too
ambitious, as in
Jesus levitated to heaven.
we wouldn't dare
elevate ourselves
to that exalted level

so, get on the elevator
you're only going to
the seventh floor.

Church

Like all mothers
church gave none other
than all she had to give

in the Sunday School building,
gruff and scary Mr. Gill
conducted children's Chapel
I didn't like him

But later seated safely
beside my daddy in church
it was all good—I belonged

only much later basking
in church's warm embrace
did she begin asking
my belief—uh, oh, time to face
the cost of belonging

God-Adam-Eve-Israel-
Jesus-crucifixion-resurrection-
Trinity-eucharist-ordination-
deacons-priests-bishops-
diocese . . .

whew—all of that?
yes that and then some
is what it costs

can I cross my fingers
behind my back
and just pretend?
is there any slack?

Well—in the pew
it doesn't matter
there, just a smatter
of attention to
all of that will do
but, you, Father, now
take your vow
take your place
fully embrace
all the niceties
of that long list

knowing that this
is the work
reserved to you
the leader
the organizer
the rabbi
(or social director?)

The Dating Service

I've tried two or three
but the feel to me
is artificiality

I've discovered
a new one recently
it begins "decently
and in order" as
they say, with
prayers, a message
focus on the leader
and formal communion

then to informal reunion
in the gathering hall
coffee and real communion
begin

perhaps a 'hookup'
might occur

Comedy

Niall* says Brits think of Parliament
as comedic entertainment
while Americans think of Congress,
as serious business

I subjected myself today to a
one hour twenty minute
presentation of five
candidates to be the
next Presiding Bishop
of my club
oh–did I mean
the Episcopal Church?
excuse me
it was serious business

near sixty-five years
I've been seriously
about the business
of being a Priest

---

* Niall Ferguson, historian, holds dual citizenship, UK and US.

on many occasions
and in many places
I've solemnly, seriously
declared that a man
was put to death
and buried on Friday
and that he was alive
again on Sunday

the whole club—seriously—
is founded on this declaration
you can go to any
local branch of this club
on any Sunday
and you'll be invited
to sip wine and eat
a little piece of paper—
I mean bread—but
it looks and tastes
like thin cardboard
(even gluten free)
And—get this—

you'll be told that it
is the body and blood
of that man who
died on Friday
and came to life
again on Sunday

I think that the Brits
idea about parliament
has merit

Jesus Reads Emily Post

A long letter from a local parish
declaims that certain things are garish
or worse, impolite to "Our Lord."
would you come late to a party
or sneak out early? My word!

And you giddy, giggling girls,
there with your jumps and whirls,
Jesus and Emily want you proper,
clearly expect you to opt for
mannerly behavior
you didn't just leave a cave or
something like that!

and one more thing—
Jesus wants you NOT to bring
your dog to this sacred place
those creatures lack the graces
that Emily so clearly praises

you may have thought you well knew
what it is Jesus wants of you.
Leviticus you may read all through.
But the complete Bible, apocrypha too,
doesn't hold Emily's cue

Proper behavior is where you begin,
using wrong fork is the very worst sin!

Defining G–d

You've noticed, I'm sure
how many are the definitions

Erasmus takes a swipe,
speaking as Folly of
*the preacher—pardon
my mistake, I would
have said declaimer* . . .

but you may go
to any church
or bookstore
or academy
or the streetcorner
and it will be declaimed
to you who g-d is
and what he (or, if you're
more modern, she)
wants, is like, needs
requires, demands

I'm weary of all these pundits
when I, myself, know exactly
who god is and her
characteristics
completely

and I'm about to tell you . . .

here goes . . .

are you ready?

First off, you can't use the name
it is too limiting . . .

ok, now . . . here goes . . .

A Debate

it is early summer '24
two clowns come on stage
one shuffles, sliding his feet
as old men do
audience titters

the other slowly appears
orange turtle shell
on his head
audience titters

a 'debate' is announced
the audience knows
it will be hilarious

a voice solemnly
announces the rules
old man, vacant stare
slack-jawed, mouth open
audience titters

the bigly man acts
bigly and stern
audience notices
his orange turtle shell
and titters

the voice poses a question
it is not about golf
orange says you can't
hit a golf ball fifty yards

old man says, 'I can, too
besides, everybody
knows you cheat'

voice poses question
old man mumbles
"about Medicare
besides everybody
knows you fuck people"
shocked voice:
sorry you can't say that
audience titters

slack-jaw continues
to mumble
orange continues
to grumble

audience laughs

voice:
"It's Saturday Night Live"
music—wild applause

And so it goes

July 4

a holiday
made for play
so, there's no
news today

turn on the TV
no news
all the business
has stopped

can we do that?

Angels

that tree in our backyard
that I love so much—
sometimes I see
angels wisping amongst
her gently swaying branches
and Abe comes to mind
invoking the better angels
of our nature

Bluewater

When the heavens are generous
they supply beautiful little
Bluewater Creek with sufficiency
to keep it happily and gently
bubbling and gurgling along.
How can we not smile and laugh
and enjoy its soft voice?

sometimes heavens are overgenerous
and little Bluewater becomes
adolescent in its temporary but
overwhelming outburst
"Don't cross me!" it roars

and there are times when
heavens become quite stingy
when our beloved
slows to a whisper

yet she remains alive
roaring, whispering
gently bubbligurgling
the process processes
continuously

that round riverrock
was there yesterday
and here today

Bluewater lives
we live
there yesterday
here today
always processing
or processing

"We shed as we pick up"
says Stoppard, in Arcadia
"Nothing can be lost"[*]

---

[*] Tom Stoppard, *Arcadia: A Play* (New York: Farrar, Strauss & Giroux, 1993), 42.

Tears

She cried only once, my mother,
maybe twice, my entire childhood
I remember my feeling—very upset
kids cry—mothers are the adults

Once at sister's birthday
skating rink party I tried
twice and fell down twice
then, head on rail, I sobbed
forever and was embarrassed
no more crying after that

we weren't criers in our family
I never saw my Daddy cry
my sister didn't cry
my little brothers cried
but they were babies
what do you expect?

Then as a hospital chaplain
and teacher, I saw plenty
of sad-making events
calling for tears

I saw, I understood the
importance of crying
but my tears didn't come
even as I so wished
there was a drought

age? mellowing? grace?
whatever. I am thankful
now my tears begin
to flow more easily
the drought is lifting

a child tries and succeeds—
the tiniest triumph
I cry

The Hallelujah Chorus
is gloriously beautiful
I cry

Leonard Cohen's Hallelujah
makes me cry

Palestinian and Israeli
children and families
suffering dying
I cry

A simple kindness is done
I cry

Jim Reeves sings
"He'll have to go"
And dies at 40
I cry as I listen

Noah Lyles crosses
the finish line first and
sets a record
Simone Biles makes
a perfect landing and
sets a record
I cry

Tom T. Hall sings of
old dogs and children
and watermelon wine
I cry

emotions
joy and heartbreak
begin to flow

Grateful for the gift of tears.

It's Never Just a Sheet

I found it in the closet
this old sheet
I did not realize that its
nicely embroidered border
was tired and frayed
when I made up my bed

I guess it's time to give
it to the ragpickers

but it is not just a sheet
Helen and I slept together
many years under that cover
I don't want Helen to go

Onomatopoeia

It sounds like what it is
Wham! Bam! Thank you ma'am!
God, I love words!

My children (and grands, too)
get aggravated when I pursue
the Latin and the Greek
derivations they don't seek

I blame Doctor Pennington
he taught me Latin for five years
for how I revel in the ways
dead Latin informs our English

I always now go to
etymology (two Greek words)—
the study of the true meaning

is this not fun?
or is it cuckoo

cuckoo, cuckoo
onomatopoeia

A Turning Point

when did your
life start getting serious?
asks the interviewer
mid-thirties country singer
several successful albums
replies

the day my son was born

L'Chaim

A Widower's Epiphany

I doubt that any housewife needs
the Myth of Sisyphus explained

Ode to the Krystal

O, you Krystal, you Krystal,
such a wonderful distil-
lation of the very fruit
of the cow, made to suit
the most discriminating taste

in Chicago the Davenport bros
saw White Castle—and said
"let's go to Chattanooga
and do our own"

A little flat square of cow
and a genius who knows how,
smother with onions, add pickle
squirt mustard—not fickle—
in steamed bun—all so delicious
almost a sin

Ms. Davenport espied
a pedestaled crystal globe
the yard art then in vogue
"hallelujah, that's it" she crowed
and the Krystal became legion
throughout all the region

at last the Davenport boys
growing tired and uninspired
sold their beloved creation
to an Atlanta corporation

Now Krystal stores
are few and far between
leaving us Krystal fans
lorn and lean

a moral, if such there be
from this sad tragedy:
brilliance does not matter
in time all crystals shatter

Hospitality

Helen lying in her bed
recovering from broken leg

Priest brings communion
and after, Helen points to
that other person in the room
ever the southern hostess
she whispers
"aren't you going to feed her?"
Becca, the priest, looks, smiles
that other person is Helen
reflected in the mirror

A Morning

The last day of August
early morning sky
covered with cotton puffs
a relief from
brutal heat of recent days

I'm outside reading
geese fly over low, honking
and a bird greets me
with a loud tweet

I'm halfway into an
incredibly moving novel
a Russian woman sniper
(309 official "kills")
novelist Quinn bases
on a true story.
harsh, war, grim, grit,
death, romance, intrigue
tears flow down my face

I am grateful,
to feel
this cool morning
and happy/sad

A Drought

Grass is brown
leaves leave untimely
birds don't sing
worms are crying

everything is parched
nothing sprouting
even I am drying up

help

The Rain Comes

my plea for help is answered
is it asking
that opens the door?

this morning I was showered
my soul refreshed
inspiration from
a speech in a play*
life is
always
universally
eternally

to life!

---

* The play is *Arcadia* by Tom Stoppard. The line: "We shed as we pick up."

I Gave up Golf Today

a gorgeous fall day is
predicted for this Sunday
I haven't played golf
since midsummer

The course has been
renovated since last
I was here.

I get a tee time—early
I'm put with a group
and anxious about it

at five til seven
a man is there
"John," he introduces
"my son and
grandson have
just arrived.

"I'm 72; you don't
look a day over
a hundred" when
I tell him my name
and claim 88

James and 8 year-old
Ryland tee up and
off we go.

they seem like nice folks
my anxiety retreats

John quits after one hole
back-spasms
oh! oh!
I'm sorry to lose him.
I'm sorry he hurts.

James, Ryland, and I
play on—five holes
and they've had enough

I'm huffing and puffing
and stubbornly keep on
pulling a cart with my clubs

I didn't even start playing golf
until I retired, and it is
something of an exaggeration
to call what I did playing golf

but for a while there was
a group of us, same level of
competence, it was fun
the camaraderie of old friends

now, new course, no group
and I've aged

long eighth hole, up hill.
enough . . .
I pick up the ball
and head home.

Filigree

Dusk,
out back on the patio
there is peace absolute
no critters speaking
no wind stirring
silence . . .

off to the side at the
edge of the little creek
that divides ours from
the neighbor is a tree
tall and full, with limbs
at the top so delicate
and slender that
they seem to me
to be filigree

a word I've never used
and not sure now it
is the right one.

I look it up
it is the right word

beauty

Good Enough

Mothers worry
'am I doing it right?'

she wants assurance
(who doesn't?)
DW—a kindly uncle*
he wants to give it
yet resists absolutes
(who is perfect?)
so he says

it is good enough

and that's good enough

---

* D. W. Winnicott, a pioneer in play therapy, coined the phrase "good enough mothering."

This Is the World*

(9/21/24)
I've only just got in my car
when my radio announces
this grand invitation
"This-is-the-world"
(important music plays)

they will go on to report
some interesting things,
specific, limited

but my mind has gone spinning off
this is the world!
everything, everywhere
wide open, limitless
"*wow*," I feel
"*yes*," I feel

then I wait to exit
the parking garage

---

* A program presented on National Public Radio

In the Garden on a Sunday Morning

CBS Sunday Morning September 29, 2024

infatuation
with a pop singer

I look at a collection of
James Bond memorabilia

Malcom Gladwell, shares with me
his quirky take on things

the leader of the Coldplay Band
lets me in on his inner self

likewise Ina Garten tells me
something about her
accidental fame

Maggie Smith died
two days ago; I get to
review her long and
glowing career

then I walk among
sunflowers in Nebraska

Walking in the garden[*]

---

[*] Based on the CBS show, *Sunday Morning*

The Sheet

I wash the sheets
make up the bed
careful to make the
covers hang straight

two nights later
they hang way far
down on my side

damn!

Helen's not here
over on her side
to keep it even

Innocent

Innocent by reason of insanity
that will never be my plea
it'll not set me free

Innocent by reason of
bad parenting is a favorite
throughout the ages
we can use that
with all the sages

It's called "trauma"
a real thing
that requires tender,
loving attention
to each one of us
we've all been
traumatized
even the
bad parents

The Rock

It didn't look very impressive
this not particularly well-shaped
rock—kind of a flat grey color

I picked it up
it was warm
in the sun all day

We walked along together
this funny-shaped rock and I
no harsh edges there
I began rubbing it
like lathering
a piece of soap

after a while I sat
down at the edge
of the field
and kept on massaging
the rock.

To my surprise
a sort of brighter
sheen began to appear
a soft glowing patina

Power

(October 7, 2023)

from here, I point
pull the trigger

fifty, a hundred
yards away
an object
falls down

total power
and
exhilaration

The Ants and the Alcoholic

parents are alcoholics
from early on, so is he
that's who he is
that's how it is to be

he wants to die

in a recovery group
downcast
looking at the floor

he wants to die

he spies ants
in line, one by one
each carrying a
tiny crumb
and then one
who is carrying
a dead ant.

it comes to him—
I can carry

Confront

A word that is fraught
as if one never ought
to come face-to-face

it may hint of hostility
and suggest fragility
in the one so opposed

or . . .
it could have the flavor
of a chance to savor;
confront could mean explore

now in my eighth decade
a different thought appears
I'm wishing now I'd made
a way to confront my fears

my father was a passionate man
without an ounce of meanness
he the grownup and I the kid
a reality behind which I hid
any impulse to confront
and so explore our relationship

thus I managed to deprive
us of the warm intimacy
of which he was surely as shy
as I

maybe it is not hostility,
but the intimacy underlying,
that we fear

Riches

Hello sadness, my longtime friend
not that I always like your trend
but you sometimes come near
and I'm foolish not to hear
what you offer me.

Hello anger, my scary friend
clearly you deserve that I attend
and stay close to see
the message you have for me

Hello happiness, my playful guide
sometimes I let you hide
when I should seek and welcome
you, and dance and sing

Oh, I almost forgot, lurking behind
anger as you always do
the most powerful one is you,
fear is your name. Come nigh
I need to look you in the eye

You all have so much to teach
and it is mine to reach
out to confront face-to-face
and fully embrace
each and all of you
as intimate friends must do.

Longing

empty
hungry
vacant
missing
not here
not there

a momentary something
I cannot begin to name
triggers the power
of the feeling

longing

those words
that word
surrounds
but cannot capture
or describe
the awareness or
the feeling

longing

longing

www.ingramcontent.com/pod-product-compliance
Lightning Source LLC
Chambersburg PA
CBHW071724090426
42738CB00009B/1866